## Cornerstones of Freedom

# The Chisholm Trail

Andrew Santella

CHILDREN'S PRESS®
A Division of Grolier Publishing
New York • London • Hong Kong • Sydney
Danbury, Connecticut

**Library of Congress Cataloging-in-Publication Data**

Santella, Andrew.
  The Chisholm Trail / by Andrew Santella.
    p.  cm.—(Cornerstones of freedom)
  Includes index.
  Summary: Presents the history of the route which became the
"Main Street" of the Texas cattle trade after the Civil War and
remained until its closing in 1884.
  ISBN: 0-516-20393-2 (lib.bdg.)    0-516-26225-4 (pbk.)
  1. Chisholm Trail—History—Juvenile literature. 2. Cattle drives—
West (U.S.)—Juvenile literature. 3. Cowboys—West (U.S.)—History—
Juvenile literature. 4. West (U.S.)—History—Juvenile literature.
[1. Chisholm Trail. 2. Cattle drives—West (U.S.) 3. Cowboys—West
(U.S.) 4. West (U.S.)] I. Title. II. Series.
F596.S232  1997
978—dc21
                               96-50144
                                    CIP
                                      AC

When the Civil War finally ended in 1865, the United States was an exhausted nation. Four years of fighting had saved the Union and ended slavery in the South. But the price of the war was high. Six hundred thousand Americans had given their lives. Survivors came home wounded or weary. Nowhere was the devastation worse than in the defeated South.

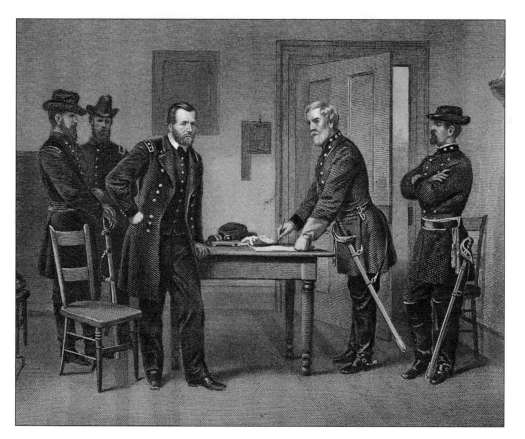

The Civil War officially ended when General Robert E. Lee (right) surrendered the Confederate troops to Union General Ulysses S. Grant (left) at Appomattox Court House, Virginia.

Even Texas, where there had been relatively little fighting, was nearly ruined by the war. Southern money was worthless. Gold and silver coins were scarce. Jobs were even more scarce. The only thing Texas seemed to have in abundance was cattle.

Texas cattle were a special breed. Their wide, sharp horns earned them the name longhorns. Their endurance made them legendary. The longhorns helped rescue Texas after the Civil War.

*The long, curving horns of longhorn cattle are their most distinctive feature.*

Northern cities were growing rapidly. Settlers were moving west. A hungry nation demanded beef, and Texas could deliver. In the two decades after the Civil War, cowboys drove their longhorns over cattle trails to the new railroad towns springing up in Kansas. The greatest of these routes was called the Chisholm Trail. It connected the open range with the railroad. It met the demand for beef in the north with the huge supply of longhorns in Texas. In the process, the Chisholm Trail helped reunite the country.

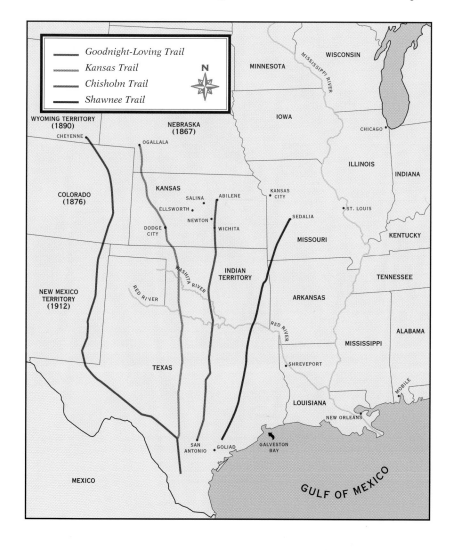

*After the Civil War, many cattle trails were established in the United States. But none was more famous than the Chisholm Trail.*

*Christopher Columbus*

The longhorns were the descendants of the Spanish cattle that Christopher Columbus brought with him on his second voyage to North America. The first cattle to reach Texas were probably brought by the Spanish explorer Francisco Vásquez de Coronado on his search for the legendary cities of gold in 1541. During the next two hundred years, Spanish adventurers and explorers made periodic excursions into Texas, bringing livestock with them. When they left, they often abandoned the animals to roam free.

*Francisco Vásquez de Coronado may have been the first person to introduce cattle to Texas.*

By 1715, the French trader Louis Juchereau de St. Denis noted the abundance of livestock left by the Spanish. The original herds had "increased to thousands of cows, bulls, horses, and mares with which the whole country is covered."

The longhorns proved to be exceptionally adaptable to their new surroundings. They were long-legged and able to walk great distances. Fending for themselves on the open range, they learned to go without water for extended periods. Their powerful sense of smell helped them to find water from many miles away. And they learned to find vegetation in even the barest landscapes. When grass was scarce they even learned to eat the leaves of mesquite trees. These were qualities that would later serve the longhorns well on the difficult cattle drives north.

*Longhorn cattle, descended from livestock left behind by the Spanish, adapted quickly to the Texas landscape.*

*Many Spanish missions in Texas had their own food and supplies, including cattle.*

By 1730, many of the Spanish missions in Texas kept their own herds of cattle. Settlers were beginning to ranch as well. The mission priests at Goliad had forty thousand head of cattle in 1770. This was the beginning of Texas's great cattle industry.

Ranchers used a variety of methods to catch and domesticate cattle. Sometimes ranchers would drive the cattle out of the brush and keep them moving until they were so exhausted that they became easy to tame. Sometimes they captured cattle by roping them. And some ranchers were not above stealing other ranchers' already-domesticated cattle.

In 1843, an Englishman named William Bollaert visited San Antonio and took note of "a rude, uncultivated race of beings, who pass the greater part of their lives in the saddle, herding

*Cowboys often captured cattle by roping them around the neck or horns.*

cattle and horses . . . unused to comfort, and regardless alike of ease and danger, they have a hardy, brigand, sunburnt appearance." He was describing the cowboy.

Cowboys were rugged, strong, and did hard work for long hours. Some cowboys were bowlegged from their endless horseback riding. They wore their hair long and often went unshaven. Even their dress was unique. Their wide-brimmed hats kept the sun out of their eyes. They wore bandannas to keep the choking dust out of their noses and mouths. For riding, they wore boots with two-inch heels, decorated with nickel-plated spurs. Their chaps were made of calfskin or goatskin.

*Cowboys were a common sight along the cattle trails.*

Every cowboy had two prized possessions. Because the saddle was a cowboy's home for many hours at a time, it was a vital piece of equipment. Equally important was the cowboy's revolving pistol, which was invented by Samuel Colt and was first used in 1839. It later became standard equipment for cowboys.

As cowboys were becoming part of the Texas landscape, the longhorn population was rapidly growing. In 1830, there were about 100,000 wild cattle in Texas. By 1850, that number had more than tripled to 330,000. In 1860, just prior to the start of the Civil War, there were more than 3,000,000 cattle in Texas.

By the late 1830s, cowboys with huge herds of longhorns were looking for new markets in

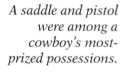

*A saddle and pistol were among a cowboy's most-prized possessions.*

which to sell their cattle. To reach these new markets, they led their herds on Texas's first cattle drives. In 1838, James White drove a herd from his ranch on Galveston Bay to the Mississippi River. Within a few years, cattle drives from Texas to New Orleans were regular occurrences. In 1846, Edwin Piper made the first big drive north from Texas, bringing one thousand head of cattle to Ohio. In the 1850s, drives north on the Kansas Trail or the Shawnee Trail were common. In fact, there were so many cattle drives that Kansas settlers soon grew opposed to them. Ticks that lived on the longhorns were sometimes passed on to the local Kansas cattle, which often became infected with and died from a disease called Texas fever. Kansans wanted to protect their livestock and to protest the presence of the longhorns. They decided to use force to keep the Texans and their cattle out of Kansas.

*The size of a herd of cattle being driven to market could range from a few hundred head to more than twelve thousand head.*

Still, the longhorns and the cowboys kept coming. In 1854, fifty thousand longhorns left Texas bound for the North. People in the big cities there were not always impressed with the breed. The first longhorns shipped to New York City were dismissed as "barely able to cast a shadow." One writer said that they "would not weigh anything were it not for their horns." The longhorns did get a chance to turn their impressive horns on their hosts. Some of them got loose and ran on the streets briefly, no doubt terrorizing the New Yorkers.

But the Civil War, which began in 1861, put an end to the long-distance cattle drives. President

*New Yorkers were unimpressed by Texas longhorns until several head escaped from a stockyard and ran through the streets of New York City.*

*During the Civil War, Union ships blocked access to Confederate ports.*

Abraham Lincoln forbade all trade with the Confederate (southern) states. The Union (northern states) blockaded Confederate ports so that ships and supplies could not get through. As a result, Texas's cattle industry was cut off from its best markets. Still, some enterprising cowboys found buyers for their beef.

A few cowboys discovered that driving their herds east to the Mississippi River town of Shreveport, Louisiana, would bring them to hungry Confederate troops. In 1862, Jim Borroum and Monroe Choate set out with eight hundred head of cattle from the Texas town of Goliad. They were bound for New Orleans. Their plan was to sell their cattle to the Confederate troops there. But as they approached, they learned that the city had fallen into Union hands. So they changed their route and headed instead for Mobile, Alabama. The longhorns had to swim 1 mile (0.6 kilometer) across the Mississippi River, but they arrived safely in Mobile.

When the war finally ended in 1865, Texas was devastated. The Lone Star State looked to the longhorns to revive its fortunes. Texas ranchers knew that there were buyers for their beef. With the war ended, they could once again sell their cattle to consumers in the big cities of the North. The ranchers also knew that the cattle could be sold for a large profit because selling prices for Texas cattle were four times higher in the North and East as they were in Texas.

But ranchers wondered about the best way to get the longhorns north. Steamboats carried goods over rivers, but they could not carry enough cattle. Railroads were being constructed in Texas, but it would take years to complete them. It appeared that the only way to get the cattle north would be to walk them overland to the railroad terminals that had already been completed in Kansas. There, the cattle could be sold and shipped to the stockyards of Chicago and other northern cities. Soon the greatest migration of domesticated animals in United States history began.

Texans started a process they called "making the gather." They rounded up stray cattle, gathering huge herds of two thousand to three thousand head. Ranchers banded together to make the cattle drive north. They combined their herds and chose a leader—a dependable cowboy who could be counted on to direct the

drive, deliver the longhorns, and bring back the money.

The trails north followed routes that had already been established by American Indians on buffalo hunts, by traders in their wagons, and by settlers moving into Texas. The trails had names like the Shawnee Trail and the Goodnight-Loving Trail. But the most legendary of all these cattle highways was the Chisholm Trail.

The Chisholm Trail was named for a trader named Jesse Chisholm. For years, he had driven his wagon up and down the trail, between Wichita, Kansas, and the Washita River in Indian Territory (Oklahoma). His wagon was a general store on wheels for the pioneers, cattle ranchers, American Indians, and soldiers who lived in and traveled through the area.

*"Making the gather" occurred when cowboys rounded up cattle for the drive north to market.*

*Jesse Chisholm*

15

*Joseph G. McCoy*

*Abilene, Kansas, was a relatively unknown town until it became a shipping point for Texas longhorns.*

But Jesse Chisholm probably never imagined that his route would become the Main Street of the Texas cattle trade. Instead, it was an Illinois cattle broker—a person who negotiates the sale of livestock—who recognized the real potential of Jesse Chisholm's trail. Joseph G. McCoy saw the need for a new shipping point for Texas longhorns and a shorter, safer route north. He found his new cattle market in Abilene, Kansas. Abilene was only six years old when McCoy first visited. It was little more than a collection of about a dozen log houses and small businesses.

But Abilene was on the railroad line that was pushing westward from St. Louis, Missouri. The railroad at Abilene would connect the ranches

and open ranges of Texas with the stockyards of the North. McCoy bought his first parcel of land in Abilene in June 1867. By September, he had built a barn, offices, and pens that would hold one thousand cattle. A bank, a hotel, and stables would soon follow. McCoy sent brochures south to Texas, advertising his new market.

The Chisholm Trail had many advantages. Because it was further west than other trails, herds on the Chisholm Trail avoided farmers who wanted to stop the passage of cattle through their land. Streams on the trail were smaller and easier to cross. There were fewer skirmishes with American Indians. In his brochures, McCoy described some of the other advantages of driving cattle to Abilene over the Chisholm Trail. "It is more direct. It has more prairies, less timber, more small streams and fewer large ones, altogether better grass and fewer flies—no civilized Indian tax or wild Indian disturbances— than any other route yet driven over. It is also much shorter because [it is] more direct from the Red River to Kansas."

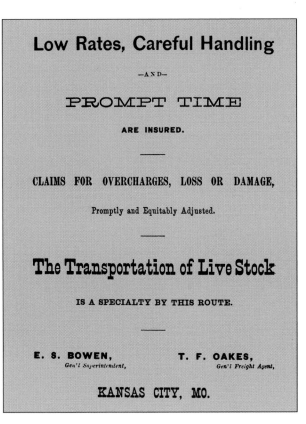

*Advertisements guaranteed prompt, efficient handling of cattle on their way to market.*

Texas cattle ranchers shared McCoy's enthusiasm for the trail. The first herd to arrive in Abilene on the new trail came even as the stockyards were being completed. McCoy's first shipment of cattle to the Chicago stockyards filled twenty railroad cars. Of the forty thousand cattle trailed into Kansas in 1867, most were driven to Abilene. There, the herds found grazing grounds and stables, and the ranchers found buyers for the beef.

Abilene's advantages proved irresistible to cattle ranchers looking for a market in which to sell their herds. In the next few years, more and more cattle drives headed north from Texas up the Chisholm Trail. Before long, a drive on the Chisholm Trail became a mark of excellence for cowboys.

Cowboys on the trail had bone-wearying work to do. Their jobs often began in the spring with the gathering of the herd. Each of the cattle were given a special brand called the road brand. A brand is an identification mark that is burned onto the animal with a hot iron. Other preparations for the cattle drive were overseen by the trail boss. The trail boss had to be an experienced and dependable cowboy because he was responsible for thousands of dollars worth of cattle. If the trail boss failed to deliver the herd in good condition at the end of the drive, it might mean financial ruin for his employers.

The trail boss was also responsible for hiring the cowboys who drove the herd north under his direction. It was crucial that the boss find the right combination of cowboys to take care of the herd. Managing a herd of several thousand cattle over a long drive took teamwork and sacrifice. The boss depended on each cowboy to work hard. Cowboys were paid between twenty-five dollars and forty dollars a month. For their salary, they rode all day, slept on the ground, weathered storms, and sometimes had to defend their lives in skirmishes with American Indians or angry farmers.

*Ranchers devised special brands that were burned onto their cattle for identification.*

The outfit's cook sometimes was paid more than the cowboys. He drove the chuck wagon, which held the supplies and provisions for cooking, and fed the cowboys. He was usually the last one asleep at night and the first one awake in the morning. Every outfit on the trail also employed a wrangler, who took care of the horse herd. Each cowboy took several horses on the drive. The wrangler's job was to be sure that the horses received proper care.

The two most experienced cowboys usually were assigned to ride point, at the head of the herd. Next came the swing riders, followed by the flank riders. Finally, the drag riders had the unenviable job of riding at the rear of the herd. Riding drag meant long days choking on the dust kicked up by the huge herds.

*The cook (standing) was a vital part of every cattle-driving outfit.*

Days on the trail started at dawn. Breakfast for the cowboys usually meant salt pork or bacon, hard sourdough biscuits, and some dried fruit.

*Drag riders covered their nose and mouth with a bandanna to filter out the dirt kicked up by the cattle and other horses.*

When breakfast was finished, the cook and wrangler packed up the provisions, while the cowboys got ready to move the herd out. At the beginning of a cattle drive, the trail boss usually liked to travel 25 to 30 miles (40 to 48 km) for each of the first few days. When the herd was well away from home, the pace might be cut back to about 10 miles (16 km) per day. The longer the cattle moved, the easier they were to handle. But the first few days, called road breaking, were the most important.

The outfit would break for dinner around midday. The longhorns grazed while the cowboys ate. But when the cattle began to lie down, the boss knew that they were finished grazing. Then it was time to get back on the trail.

The trail boss might ride ahead of the herd to find a spot near water to make camp for the

*Cattle herds were closely guarded at night.*

night. As the herd approached the spot, the cowboys would "ride them down," or gather them into a smaller and more manageable group. After the thirsty animals had watered, the cowboys would ride in smaller and smaller circles around the herd until the animals finally laid down for the night.

Cowboys usually ate beef for supper. Sometimes the meal consisted of steaks fried in flour. Other times, it might be son-of-a-gun stew, an assortment of cow tongues, livers, and hearts that were cooked together in a large pot. After supper, the cowboys took turns guarding the herd. To keep the animals calm, they might sing or hum softly as they rode. Colorful songs like "Dinah Had a Wooden Leg" and "Home on the Range" were cowboy favorites.

## "HOME ON THE RANGE"

*Oh, give me a home where the buffalo roam,*
*Where the deer and the antelope play,*
*Where never is heard a discouraging word*
*And the sky is not clouded all day.*

*Chorus:*
*A home, a home, where the deer and*
*the antelope play,*
*Where never is heard a discouraging word*
*And the sky is not clouded all day.*

The start of a new drive was an exciting time for the cowboys because of the adventure that lay ahead. The Texas prairie was lush with the new grass of spring. The patches of bluebonnets and wild mustard were dazzling. But as the days wore on the routine grew tedious. Even worse, the boredom might be relieved by unwelcome excitement. A rattlesnake might strike one of the horses, throwing its rider. Or the snake might find its way into an unsuspecting cowboy's bedroll. Worked to exhaustion and exposed to bad weather, cowboys were vulnerable to illness. In 1869, an outbreak of cholera killed two cowboys. Lightning during thunderstorms killed several others. And huge hailstones sometimes killed the animals. During the spring blizzards of 1874, one outfit lost seventy-eight horses.

But the hazard that the cowboys feared most was the stampede, which sometimes occurred when the frightened cattle tried to run away. Longhorns were known to stampede at the slightest disturbance. Anything from a flash of lightning, to the clatter of the cook's pots and pans, to a sneezing cowboy could set the cattle off and running. A short stampede might be over after a run of about a mile. After a long stampede, it could take a week to retrieve all of the cattle. Stampeding cattle could cause tremendous destruction—breaking wagons to bits and uprooting small trees. Nighttime stampedes were the most perilous. Cowboys trying to control a panicked herd of cattle in the darkness were in great danger.

Despite the hazards of the cattle drive, the herds kept coming up the Chisholm Trail from

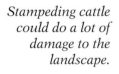

*Stampeding cattle could do a lot of damage to the landscape.*

Texas to Kansas. In 1868, 75,000 cattle were trailed into Abilene—almost twice as many as the year before. Before long, Abilene was a boomtown, with new settlers, houses, stores, saloons, a church, and a school. Abilene also attracted some of the Old West's best-known characters. James B. "Wild Bill" Hickok, the legendary marksman and army scout, became Abilene's marshal in 1871.

*Wild Bill Hickok*

Wild Bill Hickok had his work cut out for him. Abilene had a reputation for rowdiness and lawlessness that made it famous throughout the West. After the cowboys were paid, they often went to the barber for a shave, bought some new clothes, and headed for the saloon. Sometimes the rowdiness escalated to violence. To curb the violence, the townspeople passed an ordinance outlawing guns in Abilene. They posted notices of the new ordinance, but some cowboys promptly shot the signs to pieces.

It wasn't just the violence that bothered the townspeople. The cattle that were brought into town tore down fences and trampled crops. Many of the law-abiding families of Abilene decided they'd had enough of the cattle trade. They sent out a notice requesting "all who have contemplated driving Texas cattle to Abilene . . . to seek some other point for shipment, as the inhabitants of Dickinson County will no longer submit to the evils of the trade."

At the same time, the original Chisholm Trail was becoming overcrowded. One Kansas newspaper in 1871 wrote that the entire area around Salina "is filled with Texas cattle . . . and the cry is, 'Still they come.'" Cattle drives began swinging west, heading toward other Kansas towns. The Atchison, Topeka and Santa Fe Railroad was spreading southwest through the state. In the spring of 1871, two pioneers heard that the railroad was headed their way. They built a shack along the line and named their "city" Newton. The railroad reached there in July and Newton soon had a hotel, a blacksmith shop, and a saloon. Within a few years, it had a population of 1,200 people.

*By the spring of 1881, the railroad was extending rapidly through Kansas.*

The railroad brought growth to Kansas towns. It attracted the profitable cattle trade, and it attracted cowboys eager to spend their hard-earned money. A

*Posters along the railroad routes advertised an abundance of land in Kansas available for settlement.*

succession of cattle boomtowns—Salina, Ellsworth, and Dodge City—quickly sprang up on the Kansas prairie. But at the same time, other railroad lines were pushing farther south into Texas. By 1874, Texas had extensive railroad connections to St. Louis and Kansas City, Missouri. These railroads began competing for the cattle herds that once had to walk all the way to Kansas.

Other new developments threatened to end the era of big cattle drives on the Chisholm Trail. Barbed wire was introduced to Texas in the 1870s. Farmers and ranchers used it to enclose their pastures and block the passage of cattle on their way to market. The establishment of more cattle ranches on the northern plains resulted in an overabundance of cattle. With cattle available in northern regions, consumers no longer needed to look to Texas for beef. Finally, more settlers were streaming into Kansas, and as the state became more densely populated, it increasingly resisted the presence of the cattle herds. Cowboys were forced to drive their cattle further and further west in search of open land.

By 1884, the Chisholm Trail was virtually closed. Cowboys, though, did not give up. In the mid-1880s, some cattle ranchers asked Congress to establish a national cattle trail that would stretch from Texas to Canada. But the proposal went nowhere.

Still, the impact of the great cattle drives on the Chisholm Trail continued to be felt. In 1874, Joseph G. McCoy wrote that the cattle trade helped create "an era of better feeling between northern and Texas men by bringing them in contact with each other in commercial transactions." The cattle drives also helped spur the settlement of the northern plains, and sparked the growth of cities like Kansas City,

*Ranchers installed barbed wire around their land to block the routes on which cattle being driven to market traveled.*

DON'T STOP THE GAME, PAGE FENCE WILL STOP THEM.

Missouri, and Chicago, Illinois. The cattle drives also made beef readily accessible to the nation's people, and gave incentive to the railroads that eventually crisscrossed the United States. Most importantly, the cattle drives helped to rebuild Texas after the Civil War. The days of the great cattle drives on the Chisholm Trail may be over, but the spirit of the rugged longhorns—and the cowboys who drove them—lives on.

*Though the cowboys of the Chisholm Trail are gone, their impact on the cattle industry—and on the settlement of the northern plains—remains.*

# GLOSSARY

**bandanna** – large, colored handkerchief with spots or figures, usually white on a red or blue background

**bedroll** – bedding that is rolled up for carrying

**chaps** – leather leggings that are worn over jeans to protect a horseback rider's legs

**cholera** – virus in the digestive tract that can sometimes be fatal

**domesticate** – to tame

*James B. "Wild Bill" Hickok was the marshal of Abilene.*

**livestock** – horses, cattle, sheep, and other animals kept or raised on a farm or ranch

**marksman** – person who is an expert at shooting a gun

**marshal** – an officer of a U.S. judicial district who performs duties similar to those of a sheriff

**mesquite** – tree or shrub of the southwestern United States, with beanlike pods that are rich in sugar

**ordinance** – law or regulation

**outfit** – group of people who work together

**prairie** – mostly level, treeless area of land with fertile soil and covered with coarse grasses

**quarantine** – strict isolation designed to prevent the spread of disease

**range** – area of open land used for a particular purpose

*spur*

**spur** – pointed device attached to the heel of a rider's boot

**stampede** – sudden scattering of cattle or horses in fright

**stockyard** – an enclosure with pens and sheds connected with a slaughterhouse or market for the temporary keeping of cattle, sheep, pigs, or horses

# TIMELINE

**1805**  Jesse Chisholm born

**1836**  Texas wins independence from Mexico

**1846**  Edwin Piper leads first cattle drive
         north from Texas

Civil War begins  **1861**

Civil War ends  **1865**

Joseph G. McCoy
establishes
Abilene's cattle
market; Chisholm
Trail cattle
drives begin

"Wild Bill"
Hickok becomes
Abilene's marshal

**1867**

**1868**  Jesse Chisholm dies

**1871**

**1874**

Extensive rail-
road connections
established
through Kansas

**1885**  Cattle drives on
         Chisholm Trail end

**INDEX** (*Boldface* page numbers indicate illustrations.)

## PHOTO CREDITS

©: Archive Photos: 2 (Herbert), 3; Corbis-Bettmann: cover, 6, 9, 10, 12, 19, 25, 28, 30; Denver Public Library, Western History Department: 15 top, 16 bottom, 20; The Kansas State Historical Society, Topeka, Kansas: 15 bottom, 16 top, 17, 31 top, 31 bottom left; King Ranch, Inc.: 1; North Wind Picture Archives: 8, 13, 18, 21, 22, 24, 27; Stock Montage, Inc.: 26, 31 right; Superstock, Inc.: 4; The Texas Collection of Baylor University: 29; Unicorn Stock Photos: 7 (Dick Young); UPI/Corbis-Bettmann: 11.

Map by TJS Design

## ABOUT THE AUTHOR

Andrew Santella is a lifelong resident of Chicago, Illinois. He is a graduate of Chicago's Loyola University, where he studied American literature. He writes about history, sports, and popular culture for several magazines for young people. He is the author of several Children's Press titles, including *The Capitol, Jackie Robinson Breaks the Color Line,* and *The Battle of the Alamo* (Cornerstones of Freedom) and *Mo Vaughn* (Sports Stars).